Jazzy and the

Latriece M. Spires

Paige Ruiz Oramas

ISBN-13: 978-0692890660
ISBN-10: 0692890661
Library of Congress: Cataloging in Publication. Data is available upon request.
Latriece M. Spires, Allen, TX

Illustrations by Paige Ruiz Oramas
Please visit the author's website and social media pages to stay connected and to purchase additional copies:
www.latriecemspires.com
Twitter.com/latriecemspires
Facebook.com/latriecemspires
Instagram.com/latriecemspires

Meet the Author

Latriece M. Spires is a proud alumni of the University of Arkansas at Pine Bluff. She received both her bachelor's and master's in education from the historic land grant institution. She is an aspiring award winning author who developed her love for writing in early middle school. She uses her writing as an outlet to express herself in forms of poetry and short stories. She published her first children's book, "Jazzy's Big Move" in 2016. Her own childhood experiences of being bullied influenced her to write "Jazzy and the Bullies" to teach kids another way to combat the issue.

Visit her website at
www.latriecemspires.com
for more information.

Email info@latriecemspires.com
for inquiries.

Dedicated to:
To the memory of Jesse C. Thomas and Dr. Fredda Carroll and
To the many children who have had to deal with bullying.
-L.M.S.

Illustrations dedicated to:
For my husband Kelvin Ruiz Oramas
Illustrations would not have been possible without his love and support.
-P.R.O.

1

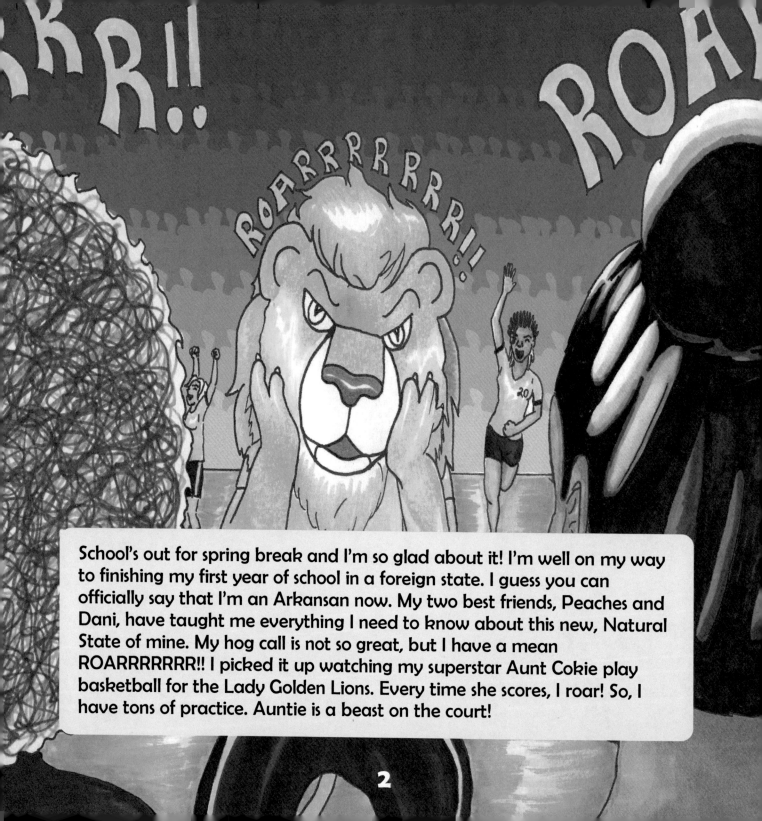

School's out for spring break and I'm so glad about it! I'm well on my way to finishing my first year of school in a foreign state. I guess you can officially say that I'm an Arkansan now. My two best friends, Peaches and Dani, have taught me everything I need to know about this new, Natural State of mine. My hog call is not so great, but I have a mean ROARRRRRRR!! I picked it up watching my superstar Aunt Cokie play basketball for the Lady Golden Lions. Every time she scores, I roar! So, I have tons of practice. Auntie is a beast on the court!

Over all, I would have to say my school year, so far, has been ok...I guess. Mrs. G is my favorite teacher. She allows us to abbreviate her last name because she is cool like that. Her hair is awesome too—soft and cottony--just like mine, but bigger. She is always chic, as fly as they come! Her class project assignments are the absolute best. She actually makes school fun. Earlier this year, we did a class project where we had to conduct a survey on ways to improve our school, according to students. We used a Likert scale to conduct the survey. A score of zero meant much improvement was needed and a score of ten meant that no improvement was needed. The Likert scale has been my go-to tool ever since. So, on a scale from 0-10, 10 being the best year ever, I would have to say that this year has been, well, five-ish so far...

I like my new school. Peaches and Dani are great; my teachers are great, and even my grades are great. However, there is a huge thorn in my side. There is a certain group of girls who don't like me. I don't bother them; I'm not mean to them. They just don't like me! I mean, these girls have no chill! Within the first week of school, they were already making fun of the way I speak. When Mrs. G. called on me to answer a question in class, the girls would mock me and giggle uncontrollably until Ms. G made them stop. Of course my accent was a little different, but it gave them no right to act so ugly! How rude! Now I know my brother Jayare works my nerves most times, but it is during these times I wished we were at the same school.

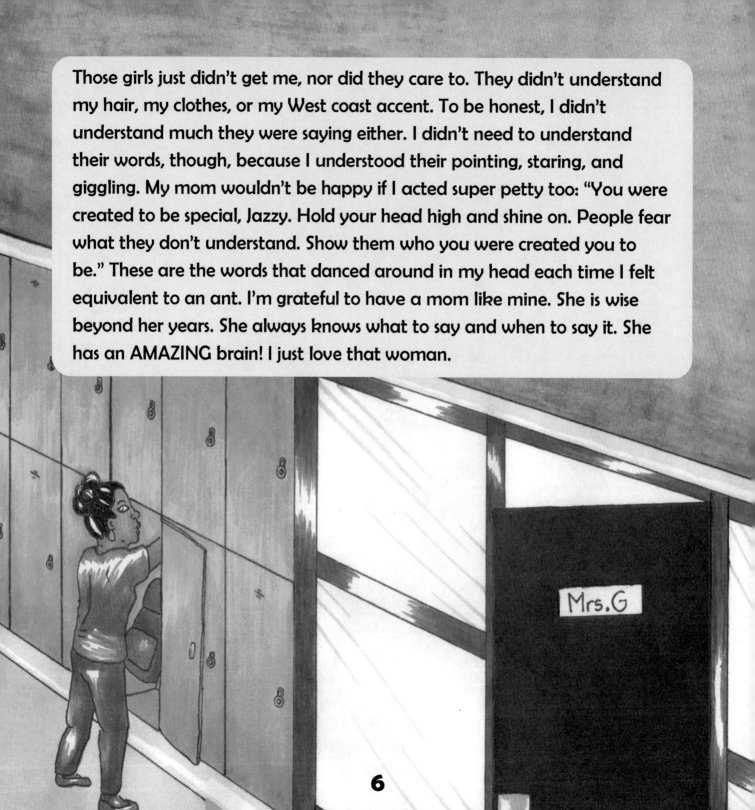

Those girls just didn't get me, nor did they care to. They didn't understand my hair, my clothes, or my West coast accent. To be honest, I didn't understand much they were saying either. I didn't need to understand their words, though, because I understood their pointing, staring, and giggling. My mom wouldn't be happy if I acted super petty too: "You were created to be special, Jazzy. Hold your head high and shine on. People fear what they don't understand. Show them who you were created you to be." These are the words that danced around in my head each time I felt equivalent to an ant. I'm grateful to have a mom like mine. She is wise beyond her years. She always knows what to say and when to say it. She has an AMAZING brain! I just love that woman.

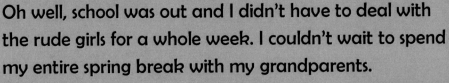

Oh well, school was out and I didn't have to deal with the rude girls for a whole week. I couldn't wait to spend my entire spring break with my grandparents. Being with them gave me a feeling of comfort. My granny's arms were the safest place on earth.

"Jayare! Jazzy! If you don't hurry, you'll miss your flight," momma warned. Waking up early mornings was the hardest. The car was packed and the sun was shining bright and Flight 1961 was calling our names. Jayare and I raced to the car, as we both were anxious to claim our favorite seat.

7

We finally arrived to the speakers above our heads screaming, "All pre-boarding passengers for flight 1961 to Oakland are ready to board." Our airport helper escorted Jayare and me to the front of the line. Our red necklaces were checked along with our boarding passes. We were seated, given wing pendants and...WHEELS UP! Yessssss! Jayare had the King of Pop blasting in my ear before we could get in the air good. His headphones were a lot bigger than mine, and so was his appetite. I saw him eyeballing the peanut butter and jelly bites momma made me because he had already swallowed his! That kid eats EVERYTHING!

It was time for our plane to land and the jazzy lady in blue took to the speaker, "On behalf of Southwest, we want to thank you for flying with us. Welcome to Oakland," said the flight attendant with the dope hair. Her hair didn't look like mine, but it was awesome! Her bun was perfect!

"Granny, Granny, Granny," I exclaimed!! I was filled with so much joy when I saw her. I ran as fast as I could as I reached for the hug that was oh-so-familiar. Jayare slowly followed behind. Even though he was as excited as I was, he was too cool to let it show. "Granny's babies!" she squealed as she hugged and kissed us and gave us one of our favorite candies from See's. We grabbed our luggage and headed for the blue Astro, the van that is. Old Blue has been in our family for many years, and if PawPaw has anything to do with it, it will be in our family for many more.

Airport security was tight, so PawPaw had to keep circling until we made our way to the pickup area. He finally spotted us waving tirelessly on the curb trying to get his attention. He scooped us up and away we flew to our family cabin in Clear Lake... ZOOOOOOOOM!

I couldn't wait to tell Granny about my BIG PROBLEM. Like Momma, she always knows what to say. I knew Granny was going to help my school year go from a miserable 5 to a perfect 10.

We made it to the cabin, dropped off our belongings, changed our clothes, and headed straight for the pier. PawPaw parked Old Blue and quickly started up the trail. The closer we got to the pier, the more aware I was of my sense of smell. It was the fishiest of the fishy...stinks so good!

We passed Aunt Mackey on our way up. She liked to fish alone and in silence. She was serious about catching fish, and she was good, too! We called her the fish whisperer. She spoke, and they listened.

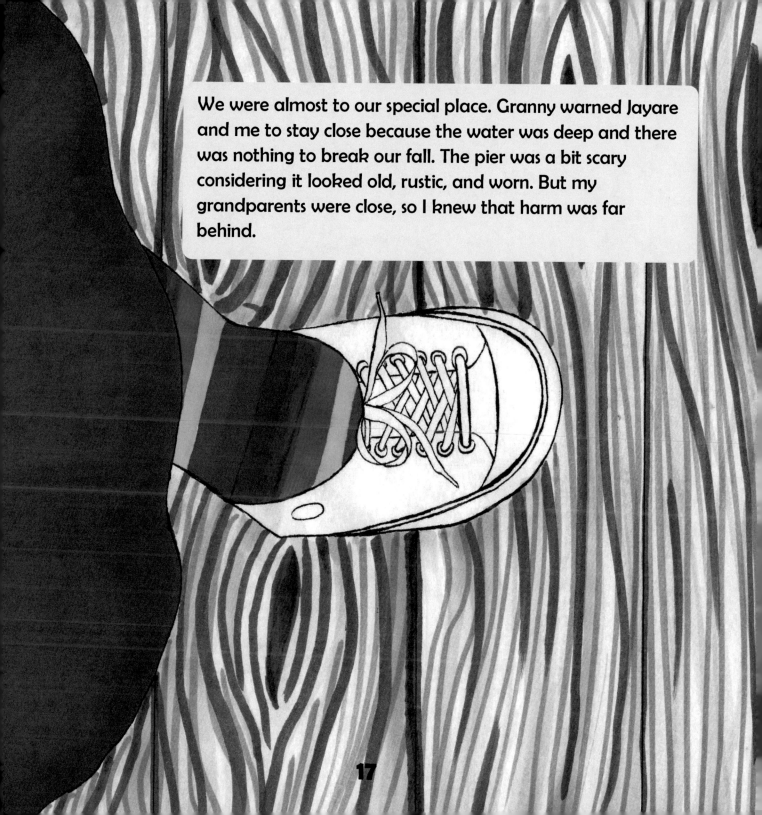

We were almost to our special place. Granny warned Jayare and me to stay close because the water was deep and there was nothing to break our fall. The pier was a bit scary considering it looked old, rustic, and worn. But my grandparents were close, so I knew that harm was far behind.

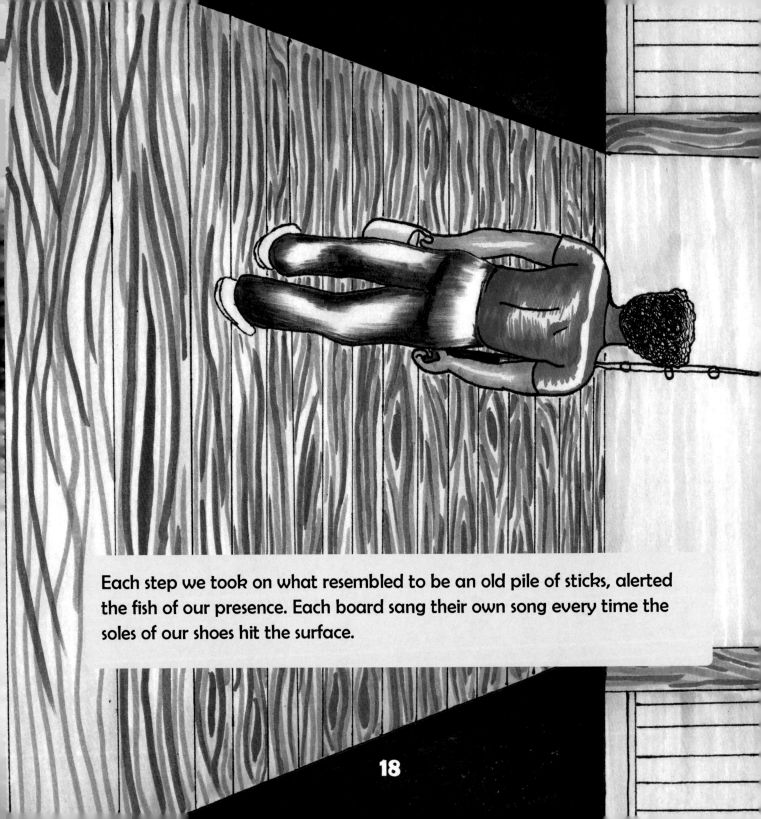

Each step we took on what resembled to be an old pile of sticks, alerted the fish of our presence. Each board sang their own song every time the soles of our shoes hit the surface.

Finally, we arrived ... 4 poles, 4 buckets, and a whole lot of time to enjoy our special spot. As we settled, I tried to focus on the fish, but my mind started to wander. Suddenly, my stomach started to do the pretzel, as if it were jamming to it's own tune. I tried my best not to think about going back to school to deal with the mean crew. But I couldn't help it. Oh, how I dreaded going back.

"Jazzy, what's the matter, Honey? Aren't you happy to be at our special place?" As my eyes started to fill to the brim, I began telling Granny all about my problems. The more I spoke, the more concerned she became. "Granny, I just want them to like me. I don't know why they are so mean. It hurts my feelings and sometimes I cry. What should I do?" I asked as the tears made their own path gliding from my cheek to my chin, and down past the collar of my shirt.

20

"Jazzy, I'm so glad you told me about your problem. You know what? I believe I have a remedy for that thorn in your side. You see baby, you have to kill 'em with kindness. In other words, don't throw a stone for a stone. Be kind to those who are mean to you. Martin Luther King Jr. once said, "Hate cannot drive out hate, only love can do that." You, my dear, are special. You must delete their mean ways with acts of kindness. People act out for many different reasons. However, you can rise above such silliness. You were created to be great, Jazzy Sparkles! You shine bright because you are a masterpiece. Don't ever let anyone make you feel less than that. You have complete control over your own thoughts and actions. When you go back to school, put on your best smile and walk tall. If the girls act ugly, take it as your opportunity to shine even BRIGHTER!"

As granny's advice played over and over and over in my head, Jayare's bobbin sunk out of nowhere! His eyes grew with excitement as PawPaw placed his hands above his to reel in the catch of the day. That was the biggest bass I'd ever seen! Many laughs, many fish, and many good meals later, our vacation had come to an end. We had a ball! I hated to leave, but I knew what I had to do.

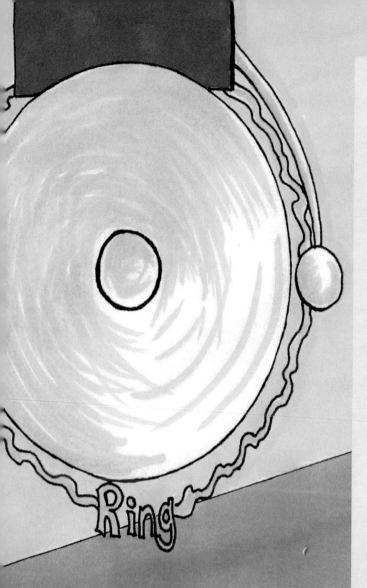

School was back in session and it was time for breakfast. As I looked over my shoulder, I could see the mean girls entering the cafeteria. At that very moment, I had a flashback of what Granny said: "Kill 'em with kindness, Jazzy." As they approached the line, I felt my heart do a mean double-dutch! I mustered up the courage, turned around with the biggest smile on my face and said, "Hello!" They scrunched up their faces as if I was speaking a different language. One girl replied "Hey, Weirdo!" The rest of her crew started to laugh. I took a deep breath and reflected once more on Granny's advice: "Shine on, Jazzy! You sparkle because you are a masterpiece."

I held my head high and said, "Hey guys, I know we've had problems in the past. However, today is a great day to change that! We can at least say good morning." I cleared my throat and let out the biggest, "Good morning! Today is a great day to have a great day!" They immediately stopped laughing. I could tell at that very moment that Granny's remedy was starting to work. I knew we wouldn't be best friends overnight. But that didn't stop my shine!

I learned a valuable lesson through all of this. I didn't have to change my clothes, my hair or the way I spoke. I didn't have to change myself one bit!!

All I had to do was change my thinking because "Hate cannot drive out hate, only love can do that." I'm well on my way to my year ending on a high note. Perfect 10, here I come!!!!!!!

Clarice Campbell has successfully counseled many children in Dallas, Texas public schools for several years. Because of her insight on the topic of bullying, she has provided a few tips as a guide for parents of elementary to middle age children.

Parents,

Bullying can be a tough subject to tackle with your children. I have provided some helpful tips of ways to break the silence.

1. Keep the lines of communication open with your children. A simple way to start a conversation with your child on a daily basis is to simply ask, "How was your day?"

2. Use encouraging words often. Your role is important in building your child's self-esteem. Allow them to participate in extracurricular activities that are important to them.

3. Teach/model good character. Because children are very observant, being kind, offering help, and having a great disposition are ways to teach/model the desired behavior.

4. Take heed to changes in your child's behavior. If you suspect your child is being bullied, notify your child's teacher, school counselor, or school administrator to help resolve the issue promptly. Common changes include: decrease in academic grades, not wanting to go to school nor participate in usual activities.

5. Take time to teach your child about the different types of bullying: cyber, social, physical, and verbal. Visit your child's school counselor for more information.

6. Teach your children what to do in case they are bullied. If possible, students should walk away and notify the nearest adult immediately.

I hope that you find these tips helpful as we continue to train our students on how to break the silence to combat bullying.

Sincerely,
Clarice Campbell

Meet the Illustrator

Paige Ruiz Oramas is an up-and-coming illustrator. She loves to breathe life into the stories she is given through illustrations using animation markers as her preferred medium. She aspires to work with her husband to author and illustrate their own children's books in the future.

Email paige.ruizoramas@gmail.com for inquiries.

Made in the USA
Columbia, SC
23 July 2017